Printed in Great
Britain
by Amazon

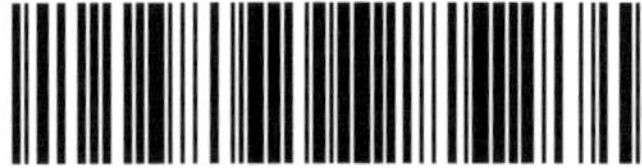

32328638R00045